Unveiling The SOUL

MARIDOL TORRES

BALBOA.
PRESS

A DIVISION OF HAY HOUSE

Balboa Press books may be ordered through booksellers or by contacting:

Balboa Press
A Division of Hay House
1663 Liberty Drive
Bloomington, IN 47403
www.balboapress.com.au
1 (877) 407-4847

Because of the dynamic nature of the Internet, any web addresses or links contained in this book may have changed since publication and may no longer be valid. The views expressed in this work are solely those of the author and do not necessarily reflect the views of the publisher, and the publisher hereby disclaims any responsibility for them.

The author of this book does not dispense medical advice or prescribe the use of any technique as a form of treatment for physical, emotional, or medical problems without the advice of a physician, either directly or indirectly. The intent of the author is only to offer information of a general nature to help you in your quest for emotional and spiritual well-being. In the event you use any of the information in this book for yourself, which is your constitutional right, the author and the publisher assume no responsibility for your actions.

Any people depicted in stock imagery provided by Thinkstock are models, and such images are being used for illustrative purposes only.
Certain stock imagery © Thinkstock.

Print information available on the last page.

ISBN: 978-1-5043-0239-5 (sc)
ISBN: 978-1-5043-0240-1 (e)

Balboa Press rev. date: 06/02/2016

Dedication

*I would like to dedicate this book
to my Dad who recently passed away,
his memory will always be cherished in our hearts.*

*My ever loving Mum;
Auntie Rosalinda and Uncle Fred.
Dearest Michael, Jenny, Colin, Belinda, Tony and Ange;
Christine, Jay, Arnold, Rachel, Anne and Amit;
as well as the rest of my family and friends.*

*Warmest heart-felt thanks for your kindness,
support, and unconditional love.*

*Also to all the beautiful souls
I've cared for during my time as a nurse;
and our loved ones who have gone before us.
Perhaps one day we'll meet again.*

To the dreamers, writers, musicians, artists,
Poets, adventurers, scientists, inventors,
Motivators, visionaries, seekers,
Carers, lovers, innovators;
And those of the future generations.

May you think with your hearts,
See with your soul and be inspired !
Never give up your search
In finding your inner truth.
And may your dreams come into fruition.

"We live in succession, in division, in parts, in particles. Meantime within man is the soul of the whole; the wise silence; the universal beauty, to which every part and particle is equally related; the eternal One. And this deep power in which we exist, and whose beatitude is all accessible to us, is not only self-sufficing and perfect in every hour, but the act of seeing and the thing seen, the seer and the spectacle, the subject and the object, are one. We see the world piece by piece, as the sun, the moon, the animal, the tree; but the whole, of which these are the shining parts, is the soul."

~ By Ralph Waldo Emerson (1803 – 1882)

More Than a Shadow

Behind every dream,
There's an individual.
Behind every individual,
There's a shadow.
Behind every shadow,
There's a story.

At times we find ourselves
Submerged in many challenges,
That we forget the wonders,
The little things that take our breath away.
The awe, the magic, our dreams
Our soul glimmering within

So regardless of the mundane,
Pause and stop for a moment.
Take a look at the shadow alongside its light,
For it reflects a great story
Which becomes alive
In your life.

Angels at Play

If you look behind you right now,
You may see eyes
With many expressions,
Watching tenderly over you.

They guide and open paths
In the hope
That you'll find your way.

Perhaps you've noticed
And probably caught their breath
As you felt a soft breeze
When humming to yourself.

Or when you're fast asleep,
The softness of a kiss
May have fallen on your cheek.

Waking you with such freshness,
A day filled with inspiration,
As sunlight peered through the window
After the rain has gently trickled down the pane.

That's when you see them
Making their way through the rays of clouds,
Moving ever so gracefully.

We only see rainbows,
But they, the angels,
Are playing
With the particles of light,

Just for you
So you, my love,
Will smile.

Spirit at Flight

At the doorstep of stars,
I entered, only to find
Endless rows of pathways

As my spirit soared
So freely
Through timelessness,

Passing through nebulas,
Coalescing into being,
Waking yet another dream,

As the Great Void
Continually sings its light
From the invisible into form.

Kisses of Light

As the moonbeam gloriously reflects
Its brilliance over a calm, deep lake,

Hearts opened like a lotus
To each other's glow,

Allowing kisses of light to flow,
Illuminating and warming our souls.

As our souls drink
From the same life force,

Freeing all shadows into light,
Remembering, renewing, revitalising.

Whole and complete,
With kisses of light in our hearts - overflowing.

Interwoven

There you were
As if in a dream,
Like a glimmer of spark
Amidst the haziness
Of a memory,
Ephemeral.

There you were
As if in a picture
Within the shadowy stillness,
Through lingering thoughts
Never forgotten,
Enigmatic.

Moments captured in time
Of tears, passion, and endurance.
Warm smiles and laughter
As your being, and that of mine,
Will always be
Interwoven.

Dear Butterfly

There was such agony in the world,
Yet the butterfly continued to absorb beauty
As it transformed pain into colours,
The multi-speckled patchwork
Keeping its wings at flight.

At night it released its anguish
As it left butterfly kisses
On dewy blossoms,
To be transformed
By the warmth of morning light.

As the days went by,
The sun shone brighter.
The butterfly graciously thanked the world
For allowing it to feel eternity,
In its momentary existence.

Heart Aglow

Silent being
Of formless light
Kindling a glow
Brighter than the sun,
Filling you with luminance
From the inside out,
And the strength
Which gives wings
To your heart.

Book of Light

Endless pages
Inscribed by light
Are filled with the etchings
Of memories.

The interplay of beings
And life forms
Experiencing many realities,
From the seen to the unseen,

All occurring simultaneously,
Linked and interwoven
From chapter to chapter
Within your book of light.

Flow of Change

Change
Letting go
New beginnings
Regeneration

Two hearts coalesce
Stars collide
New life
Growth

Sorrow
Exhalation
Pain shed
Unbound freedom

Clarity
Eyes bright
Arms outstretched
Rebirth

Motions at Play

Spindles of a dream
Are spun through light,

Scattered by the winds,
Reflected by the stars,

Danced by our souls,
Like fire-flies in synchronicity.

Motions of serendipity
Wondrously ablaze.

Hold On

When there are too many challenges,
And you feel that you just can't go on,

Hold on.

When the world closes doors
And shuts you out because you're different,

Hold on.

When everything you do
Seems like a never-ending maze,

Hold on.

When your feelings and voice seem unheard
In spite of doing your best,

Hold on.

For it is all momentary,
Like the clouds in the sky.

Hold on.

Every moment has a gift of wonder,
Laid upon the many paths of your destiny.

Hold on.

Strength

Gentle being,
You are one,
Yet you speak for many.

You give voice
To silent thoughts
Ashamed to be expressed—

Feelings and yearnings
Discouraged and belittled,
Shunned and ostracised,

But you open insights
From eyes
Beyond the flesh,

Expressing what truly matters,
Seeing with the heart
Of the soul.

Dream Keeper

She, within
The ancient rivulets of light
Resides in dreams,

Where the trees
Of inspirations bloom
Vibrantly, wild and free.

She was by your side
During childhood,
Igniting your curiosity;

The awe, magic, and wonder,
Adding that certain kind of spark
To your life.

She was there as you sent
Your hopes with the wind,
Whispers carried to the moon and stars

As she nourishes the streams of dreams,
Warming your heart
With an inflow of love.

Inscribing Light

Within the solace of your room,
Being filled with anticipation,
Arched over pen and paper,
Eagerly writing.

Wind chimes sway
In the distance
As angels play
Its tunes.

Streams of insight
Flood your entire body
Like a vessel,
Inscribing light.

Pages after pages
Come alive
As expressions pour
Across the blank sheets,

Unravelling your book,
Your heart songs,
As the music of your soul
Began to sing.

Eternity

I AM
The indivisible spark,
Moving all manner of creation
From the unseen to the seen.

I AM
Eternity connecting star to star,
Permeating from the vast emptiness
To which all came to be.

I AM
In light
The spirit in you and me,
The all-encompassing glow of Divinity.

Inner Spirit

I recognise you anywhere,
Regardless of the essences you embody.
I see the radiance of your heart
Filled with ancient knowing
And future wisdom,
Alight with a thousand dreams,
Ready to light up in countless possibilities.

You sometimes forget who you are
As you search outside yourself.
But all along,
You are always connected
To universal energies
Which dance and sing
All the stars into being.

There is peace beneath your breaths,
Great warmth surrounding your presence,
An aura not seen by all.
And as you laugh with such deep joy,
Luminescent wings arch
Their splendour and grace
Towards the sky.

Ethereal Rose

I've seen the depths of your tendrils
Dug deeply into the soil, yearning to reach out

With hopes and dreams,
Nestled in pain through the drought

Amongst thorns and thistles
And branches which barbed and choked,

As welts of rain and the freezing frost
Overwhelmed your blossoms.

But as the sun shone through,
You inhaled its glow in every pore,

Eventually stretching and reaching out
To raise your brow to the sky,

To unravel the cords
And breathe in the horizon of spring,

Dressed in the most crimson of reds
With an aroma etched in my memory.

Your presence was brief
As winter approached,

Yet in your silence,
I felt your love,

Knowing that you're always there,
My ethereal rose.

Misunderstood

Felt your deepest pain
As you wept silently

Through glossy eyes
That saw beyond a wider scope.

The eye of the beholder
Looking out, looking in;

Feeling deeply,
Seeing so much;

Hard to fathom,
But understood by the soul.

Seer

A traveller
Journeying home
Wore his earthly belongings
Like a musty old coat,

The material possessions
That weighed him down.

With each stride taken,
He reluctantly approached
The archway
Of his destination.

Winds of impermanence blew,
Gradually stripping him down,

Revealing his nakedness,
His true identity:
The seer of the soul,
Looking out.

Transitions

Journeying
After completion.
Yet to another existence,
Multitudes of lights are everywhere,
Gliding beyond layers of space-time,
Travelling into eternal vastness
Through the portals of eternity,
To different realms,
Connected
To all.

Stripped

When stripped down
To the core of ourselves,

We find

That we are pure energy,
Spirits in their boundless interplay

Song of the Cosmos

Choirs of light
Sing their songs
To stars
And pierce the great darkness
With their endless chords,

Sparking the great void
That unleashes galaxies
Into a tumultuous pirouette,
Whirling worlds into form
Upon the stage of existence—

A cascade into the templates of life
As songs of the cosmos
Continually play
Luminescent melodies
Deep from the heart of eternity.

Cycles of Existence

From invisibility,
There is substance.

From complexity,
There is simplicity.

From the ordinary,
There is the extraordinary.

Within the existence of the microscopic,
The macrocosm of the universe is mirrored.

Where there is movement of time,
There is none.

That which is linear
Dynamically and progressively cycles.

From the cycle,
That which is chaotic,

Orderly,
Returns to invisibility.

Weeping Rain

Driving.
Heavy rain pelting,
Blinding my direction.

Disorientated.
The road narrowed;
My vessels constricted.

Lost.
My heart started to beat faster;
My breath became tighter.

Fear
Filled my mind
As hot tears fell uncontrollably like the rain.

Vulnerable.
I felt blinded
As the road blackened in the distant.

Alone.
Didn't feel like I belonged anywhere,
Felt utter loneliness.

Lights
Flashed from behind as cars passed by,
Like souls at their wakes, on their paths.

Bewilderment
Overwhelmed me. "Where am I going?" I yelled.
My airway tightened; my limbs felt weak

Hurt.
As I felt immense pain,
The heartache of slowly letting go.

Knowing
I had to find calm,
I had to find my way home.

Courage
Eventually filled my being as I mustered the strength
To quieten the noise that circled my mind.

Sighs.
With each deep inhalation,
Light filled my lungs.

Trail.
I found a way that looks familiar.
I wasn't quite home, but I'm on my way.

Heart Flow

If you were to peer
Into your heart,
You would see it light up
Like billions of stars
Being born,

Imbued with a song,
Sparking its flow
As your soul
Sings its countless melodies
From sadness to joy.

Phoenix

I saw you
In the corner of your room,
Head down
With your hands over your head,
Crying endlessly.

You were so confused,
Felt so alone and misunderstood;
Countless challenges overwhelmed you.
Hours turned to days,
Days to weeks, and weeks into months.

The agony seemed endless,
As if shunned in a shell.
You didn't want anyone to enter;
You felt it safest to lock everyone out,
Building the highest walls around you.

As you felt hurt,
Fear created a prism around you
Of anger and despair,
Basting your being with its disdain,
Far from whom you really are.

Through this most weakest and vulnerable moment,
It somewhat dawned on you
That you've just hit rock bottom!
Now everything started to shudder
As clarity pierced through the pain.

Realisation has began
To fill your being.
It was time
To peel the mask
And arise!

Within the silence of your room,
You heard the whispers
Of your inner voice, as loud as can be,
Yearning to speak its truth
From your innermost core.

And through glazed eyes,
You managed to see
Past the façades,
Like eyes alight
In complete darkness.

You saw the wondrous radiance
Reflecting vibrantly from inside out,
Through every molecule and cell
And all that's in between,
Dissolving the dimness within.

Gratitude overwhelmed you
As clarity filled your eyes
Like diamond specks of light,
Grateful to feel and empathise,
To understand, forgive, learn, and cherish

You carried yourself out of the darkness,
Awakened like a phoenix inhaling its first breath
With wings outstretched to their fullness,
Capable of rising above any circumstance,
Allowing the magnificence in you to shine!

Moving Forward

I set my pain free.
I set you free.
I wipe my eyes.
I get up.

Pick up the pieces.
Pick up my bags.
Pick up what's left of me.
Pick up my life.

Releasing hurt.
Releasing lies.
Releasing fear and suffering.
Releasing tears uncontrollably.

Feeling strength as my knees shake.
Feeling the eagerness of moving forward.
Feeling integrity and self-worth.
Feeling my inner being, reclaiming its life.

Tears

Oh, caterpillar,
Please don't cry.

If only you know
Just how magnificent

You're going to be
As a butterfly,

Free to flourish
Beyond the endless anguish,

A chance to unravel
Those glistening wings

That finally ascends you
To your most cherished dreams.

Seeds of Hearts

Allow your heart to open
And be kissed by light,

So that it blooms
And overflows with luminosity,

Endlessly flourishing
The seeds of hearts.

Serendipity

Brought forth
From eternity
Into an awakened dream

Are souls
Alight in all forms,

Singing stardust into being—
Hopes and longings
Into serendipity.

Savour

Savour
Every moment,
Being in its presence
Memories splicing reality,

For it will become
As it was once again:
Luminescence
Within a dream.

Going Before Your Time

You are unwell,
Going before your time
As you're stricken with an illness
That ravages, and takes your sustenance—
Depletes, robs, overwhelms, nauseates.

Each day, I feel you slowly weaken;
The ache and sadness in your heart,
Your worries, hopes, and longings,
As your limbs lose their strength
And your hair slowly falls away.

To me, you will always be
As beautiful as you are,
Unchanged with time,
Never forgotten,
Forever loved.

Angel's Embrace

Tears fall, but it's time to gently wipe them away;
There's no need to fear or worry.
Warmth and blessings
Surround you,

Filling you with the deepest comfort

As arms of angels
Encircle and embrace you,
Filling your soul with a glow,
A splendour of deep calm.

For angels sing the most glorious songs

As they guide and take your hand
From light to light
To eternal love
And life.

Unbound Serenity

Through an invisible archway
Where time does not exist,
Immense peace and light
Surround and fill me.

All my pain, sorrow, and tears
Are wiped away,
No longer ridden with disease,
Suffering, or remorse.

Thoughts that are never spoken,
That will never be expressed,
Are understood on the other side,
The place where destinies align

I now stand weightless,
Fearless and set free,
Beyond measureless sight
In an ambience of unimaginable serenity.

Your Travels

You've ventured through many roads,
Crossed many seas,

Peeled away
Layers of sorrow

Embedded into the attire
Worn throughout your travels.

Each decade led to centuries
As you've continued on,

Voyaging through
Many dreams,

Each time releasing a fragment
Of yourself,

Coiled like glistening threads
From deep inside your soul,

Trying to find its way
Across the dark void

Which unravels the pathway
Leading home.

Sanctuary

At last,
When it is time,

You will see
That which you've always longed,

As the roads ahead finally align,
Lighting up your way home.

All will ultimately be revealed
In a boundless place of sanctuary.

Mirror of My Soul

We've met before
Many hundred years ago,
On the outer skirts of our dreams.

We've lived in the past,
Present, and future at the same time,
As we watched shooting stars go by.

Wishes have come true
Like a dream in a dream
That became reality

As we met again and again,
Gazed into each other's eyes,
And remembered.

Hearing your heartbeat,
The signature in its tone;
Your voice, scent, and touch are always familiar.

Together we've held hands
In the many corridors
Of eternity.

Our souls reflected back
At each other
Like the mirrors of time,

Jewelled memories
Unwinding from an endless chasm
Filled with light.

Soul to soul,
Heart to heart,
In unison within a shared destiny.

Wherever we are,
We shall always meet,
Caring for one another,

Always venturing together
Within the boundless rivers
Of infinite stars.

Beside You

It is here
That I've come to be
Along beside you.
As you called my name
From the depths
Of your soul,
I heard every heart thought
Through the drumming
Of your pulse,
Your longing, and your pain,
Your hopes for joy,
And dreams yet to unravel.

It is here
That I've come to be
Where spirit is real
And expressed
In a journey
Right beside you;
Where blossoms
Flourish and thrive,
With every heartbeat,
Opening light-filled passages
As destiny unfolds
Within the palm of eternity.

The Garden of Stars

I'll meet you
In our garden,
Where all that is old and new
Converges as one.

Be there for me
As the gaze of light
Falls on unfolding space—
Delicate crossroads that turns into paths.

It is there
That I'll greet you
With arms wide open,
Like a dove

Gently uncurling its wings
So as to enfold
Two edges of time
In an embrace of a shared destiny,

As we feel the divine
In every breath,
Our hearts beating
Within our souls.

Convergence

Convergence
Of souls
Alive in the other,
Reunited.

Hand in hand,
Heart to heart,
Flesh to flesh,
Lips to lips.

A bond beyond the stars,
Like galaxies
In their entwinement,
Loved.

The Day We Met

We met at the crossroads
Where stars began,
Waiting for our melodies
To play.

Together we sat cross-legged
With curiosity and awe,
Fervently watching the cosmic dance
That brought us into being—

The weaving of melodic light
As it moved its way
Into the seams,
Connecting all,

Leaving imprints of beams
Etched into the blueprint within our souls,
A mosaic of memories that are always there,
Finding its way into our hearts throughout eternity.

In Oneness

Listening
To the pulses
Of your heart.

Sacredness
Coming alive
From timelessness.

Breathing
Breaths of light
Into heart rhythms.

Dwelling
In oneness
Within our cores.

Pathways of the Heart

Woven

Into timelessness

Are the soulful strings

Between your heart

And mine.

Tenderness

Inhaling deeply
As the wings
Of my heart
S-t-r-e-t-c-h-e-s
To its fullness,
Lifting me
To boundless sights.

Exhaling
With your breath
And seeing
That my soul's eyes
Are yours,
Our every motion
Like music.

So many sensations
Fill our vessels
As energetic rays
Surround us.
Heartbeats merge,
Feeling complete
In the arms of love.

Basking in Love

Within
The nakedness
Of my heart,

I swim with you,
I make love with you

In its streams
Of boundless
Eternity.

Heart Trails

There lies
At the heart
Of the universe

Pure love,
Pure light,

In its myriad
Interconnectedness
To all.

Secrets of Time

After the first spark of light,
When the horizon is just a haze,
I feel like a person born between time,

Carrying within the secrets
To a place where time does not exist.

Each day, each month, each year goes by,
Sleep after sleep,
Ticks after tocks.

Every second forward is a second gone by;
As I move to the future, I step to tomorrow's past.

One step forward,
Another stepped back.
It's like dancing by standing still.

Is the clock a façade, disguised to fool all?
As one hundred years go by, two hundred, and more,

Am I to be of the past as seen in the future?
Or of the future as seen today?
Am I to be here again, or elsewhere?

Clairsentient

Your eyes—
Big and black
Like dark matter,
Windows of the cosmos,
Absorbing.

Clairsentient,
Enigmatic,
A conundrum,
Intangible,
Misunderstood.

Seeing through
Beyond time,
Feeling,
Experiencing,
Transforming.

Your Voice

Echoes
Of your love

Unfolding
In the depths of stillness,

Brightening
The darkness along my path,

Inspiring
My direction and event strings,

Guiding
From a deeper voice within.

Destiny's Plight

Surrendered,
Held, and lifted,

Carried by the arms
Of destiny,

Not knowing the direction,
Which way to go,

Just following
The compass within.

Worlds after worlds
In spheres of dimensions,

A millisecond
In the grand experience,

Filled with pathways—
All leading home

Into the oneness
Within eternity.

Blockages

Fear hinders and stagnates
Like a heavy rock,
Weighing us down.

But as it is recognised,
We release the blockages,
See things for what they are,

Setting our spirits free
The light of who we really are
Into such clarity.

The Sleepy Sun

Something was different about today.
Immense energies filled the air
As I sat on my favourite cosy chair
At home by the beachside.

I watched the seagulls swoop to find food
As hundreds of wings glide by,
Casting their shadows on hill-mounds
Ever so vibrantly free.

As noon approached,
Strangers made their way home
Just like the hundreds of birds that were at flight,
Winged splendour gradually descend to shelter.

I too am ready for sleep.
My heart felt like it was being filled with light,
Allaying any fear and sadness
As I exhaled my very last breath.

The feeling of grace
Enveloped me with its warmth—
An all encompassing embrace
As eternity welcomed me home.

With outstretched wings,
I flew afar
Into the open arms
Of pure love.

Together
At last,
It was time
For rest.

Resplendence

With exhilaration,
My heart expands,
Sensing the gloriousness
Expressed through every life force
Like a continual respiration of light
Grateful to flow in its currents,
Absorbing such resplendence,
Experiencing the aliveness
Of being and form
And indivisibility.

Our Home

Many envision thoughts
Echoing a strong desire
For calm to embrace
Earth.

It is the energy
Radiating
From billions of individuals'
Minds,

Connecting and sharing
Hopes of optimism
For nature, the wilderness, and
Humanity

To resume
A level of balance
Within our innermost
Beings

As it reverberates
A longing for change,
Harmony, and
Peace,

Which ultimately returns home
Where it once begun—
Simple kindness from an individual's
Heart.

Nature

Her voice is echoing elusively
As Mother Nature sings her tunes
From deep within the soil
And through empty space,
Connecting,

Signalling
Changes and new growth
As great energies circulate,
Setting motions at play
Harmonising imbalances, and its flow.

Deepest Thoughts

I saw you sending
Heart-thoughts
To the stars,
Where they flowed

Into the heart

Of the universe,
Where dreams awaken
And destiny unfolds
Yet another reality.

Other Worlds

Each evening as I look up
Deep into the darkness of night,

I see the brilliance of stars,
A countless number of suns
Just like our own,
Filled with dreams,
Land, and shores;
Sentience at its wake.
Looking up at their sky above,
Pondering the possibilities of life.

Each evening as we look up,
Deep in awareness, we unite.

Weavers of Time

Every so often,
Woven into awareness

Through the furrows
Of consciousness,

Are the insights of sentinels,
Guardians within the cosmos,

Bringing vision alive
Through heart-thoughts

Allowing untold daydreams
To meet its preceptor.

Emergence

Viewed
Through the passages
Of the arrow of time
Is the past, present, and future
Occurring in the now;

Seemingly happening
At different intervals,
Places, spheres, and dimensions
As space folds itself
Into the valleys, peaks, and troughs
Of boundless possibilities
Laced with the fabric
Of quantum entanglement
Fastened by light;

Gathered into the seams
Of a woven mesh
Cast by a Viewer
At the outer rim
Of space-time.

Canvas of Being

There's always a bigger picture
To a bigger picture

When we see
With our hearts,

The boundlessness
Within and throughout

Illuminating our thoughts
Beyond current perceptions,

Setting ourselves free
In the ocean of possibilities,

As each day we paint
The canvas of our being with light.

Glow to Glow

I feel the glow of the sun
Gently warming,
Leaving a wisp of a kiss
Against my cheek.

Vibrant energies fill the air,
Generating spring
From beneath the roots
To the sky.

I'm totally in its dance
As chords of melodic light
Encircle me,
I feel enlivened, and in its bliss!

Blossom

Don't be afraid
To blossom
Into the truth
Of who you are
And your heart's vision.

The fleeting moments
Of anticipation and fear
Eventually disappears,
Just as the petals
Afloat on a glistening lake.

Alone

You feel so alone
That everything
Is falling apart.
As you doubt yourself,
The things you do,
The hopes you have
Are shattering
Into tiny thousand pieces,
Fragments scattering
Just before your eyes.

Nothing is left
But the tears that fall
Across your face,
And confusion drowns your mind
As you heave deeply
The sigh of pain,
Cutting into wounds,
Into the bare flesh
Of sores that weep
With agony through the dark.

The Release of Pain

Loss
Hurt
Isolation
Abandonment

Pain
Anxiety
Anger
Neglect

Grief
Confusion
Misunderstanding
Ostracised

Uncertainties
Judgements
The list goes on and on.
It never seems to stop!

I yell for it to go away.
I push it away.
I cry in the darkness, in my sleep.
I cry on your shoulder, alone.

I search within the emptiness.
I search in eyes that stare blankly
In crowded streets,
In busy parks and barren beaches.

Endless noise swirls through my mind,
Flooding it with clutter and confusion.
My eyes peer, but my presence is hardly there.
Does anyone understand?

I yearn, I long for someone, something
To hear me, to be there,
To listen, to empathise
As my heart aches.

I'm here but feel separate—
No sense of belonging.
I would really prefer
To be elsewhere,

Anywhere else but here,
As I never feel at home anywhere.
Where's the door for me to exit?
To open? To exist?

I've searched outside for so long.
Now I'll search within.
That's the only way
My heart will be my guide.

Through wiped eyes
I shall unravel those knots and binds
As if peeling the bandages
From a chrysalis, setting myself free,

Seeing the present
Within every unfolding moment
Of life's uncertainties,
As it is all right to feel and cry.

For I am
Innocence
Empathy
Kindness

Understanding
Perseverance
Wisdom
Mystery

Gratitude
Compassion
Courage
Hope

Truth
Passion
Possibilities
Wonderment

Creativity
Serenity
And above all
I am love.

Dissipation

Walk with me
Through to the other side,
Where the air is fresh.

Meeting new challenges
Circumstances that come and go,
Like the waves lapping the sea.

Past all anguish and woe—
The suffering carried by the hands
Of impermanence.

Blissful Observer

Ethereal being,
Formless and timeless.

The inner flame
In you and me.

Pure love and light,
Eternal.

Blissful observer
Within.

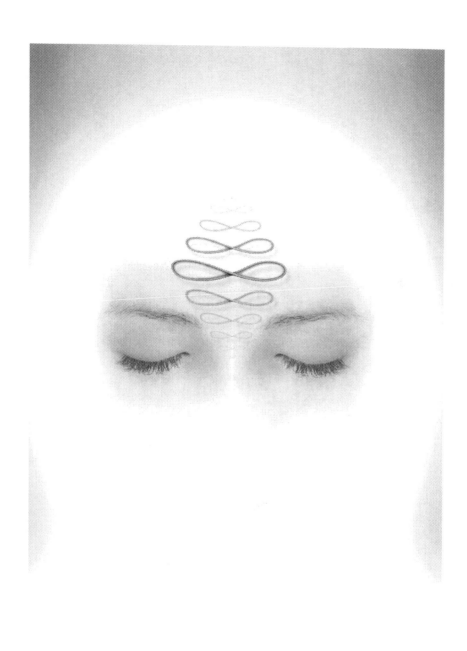

Luminosity

Luminosity
Cuts through mind and heart;
Fear, resentment, and stagnation;
Embers and ashes
Scorched by pain.

Luminosity
Cuts through the emotions held like a bud,
Afraid of the shadows and the dark
Unravelling the petals,
Setting it free.

Unfurling its splendour in full bloom
Revealing its truth,
That inner self
Radiating:
Luminosity.

Hurt

I feel your hurt,
The rawness of your being,
Your vulnerabilities and pain,
Hidden behind a smile.
I sense your dismay,
The loneliness,
As you try to make it
Through the night.

Never give up. Never give in.
Take each day as it comes.
There is a deeper meaning within you
That's unique to yourself,
Unbound peace within your core.
Connect with that, and for all you know,
Something great is already on its way,
Just around the corner.

Reconnecting

Forgotten,
Walking like a shadow,
Watching the world passing by
As if buried ten feet under.

Too many distractions;
Noise pollution fills our thoughts:
Expectations, dramas, façades,
Meaningless work
Are vibrating us away
From who we really are—
Our core values,
Our true goals

Drifting us away from really seeing,
Hearing, and feeling
Experiencing the moments. Each other.
Reconnecting to the aliveness of being.

Walls

The only thing
That separates us

Are the walls
Of our perceptions;

The quagmire of thoughts
Shooting at the enemy;

Bullets of anger and hatred,
The silent killer,

Unleashing its venom,
Poisoning inside.

Forgiveness

Emotions
Instilled in our cells,
Tissues, minds, and bodies,
Which corrode and fester.

A lifetime of toxic patterns
That continually hurt
Brought down through the passage of time,
When all you really want is peace.

Events that stung and burned
Through the lining of a scar,
Embedded deeply in your heart,
Tormenting you senselessly

As you held on to the triggers
Worn like your identity,
A garment tethered to endless cycles
Basting you with intense agony.

Forgiveness
Is a source of freedom
To allay the pain and finally set it free,
To start anew.

As you set your intention
To truly let go. Cut the cords.
A complete cleansing,
Revealing the truest you.

The Flow

Untangle
Knots
That solidify,
Hinder, and stagnate

Flow.
Live
Like you're alive
In thought and action.

Revive.
Breathe.
Arch your chest to the sky.
Reignite the zest within.

Soar,
Extend
Those graceful wings,
And set your spirit free!

For Those I Cared For

Every now and then,
I feel your presence around me:
The hundreds of beautiful souls
Whom I respect and cared for
As a nurse and a person.

As I remember holding you in my arms,
Feeling your vulnerability,
Your utmost pain,
Seeing through
To your ageless being.

Past the illness,
Disfigurement, or disability.
Feeling your tenderness through those tired eyes,
Even when you felt ashamed,
When you couldn't speak.

You are never forgotten,
For one day we shall all meet again
In that boundless realm
Where words are not needed,
And our wings take flight beyond.

Being Yourself

It's alright to be vulnerable.
It's alright to be kind.
It's alright to follow your heart.

It's alright to be unique.
It's alright to be yourself,
Just as you are.

It's alright to speak your truth.
It's alright to make a change
And a difference in someone else's life.

Set Free

Crush those walls
From around your heart.
Release your fear and suffering.

Set them free
Like wings vibrantly at flight
From your innermost core,

Carried into the expansiveness
To that which threads all
With light

As it returns
To unravel your dreams
Through signs and synchronicity.

For in every corner that you turn into
Is a reality
Waiting to start anew.

Formless Light

Gentle being
Of formless light,
Filled with kindness
And unconditional love,
Caring selflessly. Always there.
That which you've shared
Is forever treasured,
As you'll always
Remain a part
Of our being
And within
Our hearts

Remembrance

Cherish
That which is expressed
Through the light
Of your soul,

As one day
When you look back,
It'll be the things
That really count the most.

DeLight

Feel, express, appreciate.

Rejuvenate.

Let go.
Delight in the wonder
Of existence.

Flourish.

Receive, re-create, renew.

The Wake

In an awakened dream,
We soared beyond time,
Connecting and rejoicing,

With the Divine—

Source of all,
Infinite light,
Love of my soul.

Memories

Memories woven in time and space,
Coalescing into form,
Fleeting moments
Held by a reality,

A thought of a thought
By the Infinite,

Leaving tracks of light,
Blueprints of eternity
Remembered by the soul,
Memories woven in space and time.

Inner Knowing

There are moments
When we feel so centred,
Profoundly connected
To those around us,
The rhythms of nature,
Universal energies,
The life force in all.

We feel our being
Glistening within,
Innate knowing
Living its truth,
Soul essence within flesh,
The inner observer—
Alive.

Sun Within

There's a vibrancy
That shines from within;
Its glow is brighter than any sun.
It can never be extinguished
Or ever taken away from you,
For its brilliance refracts
The darkness in sight.
So as eternity
Is seen
In all.

GLOW

Release
Versatility
Flow!

Stretch
Resilience
Glow!

Breathe
Relax
Appreciate!

Star
Light
Heart!

Remember
Soul
Shine!

Make a Wish

The voice within
Sang songs without words,

Like wishes made
In silent thoughts,

Then seeing them
Come true.

It moves you
With such wonder and awe

As it unravels events
That take your breath away.

My heart sang its songs
In a language hard to comprehend,

But understood by the stars
And translated by my soul.

Perceptions

In silence,
As I read this book,
Perceptions starts wandering.
Thoughts race through my mind
Beyond the countless oceans
Of awareness and wonder
Into other states
Of imaginings.

Pathways

All visions,
Heart-thoughts
Unspoken words
Are heard in the realm
Of invisibility.

All are transformed
By light,
Unfolding pathways
Awakened
By destinies,

For you to choose
As you lay
The foundations
And express the voice
Of your heart.

Gaia

There is a raging battle
Within my body:

Disharmony
Of an extraordinary kind.

Silhouettes in armoured gears
Of troops and their bleeding hearts.

Never-ending cycles
Throughout the ages of time.

As concrete jungles
Reach higher towards the sky.

Out of control,
Suffocated land. Dying sea.

Dis-eased. Unrest.
Endangered.

Planet Earth—
Koyaanisqatsi.

Harmony

A thought
From one person,
Echoed by millions,
As yearnings and longings
Of hearts encircle and fill our globe,
With an undeniable hope
Encompassing harmony
In this unique world
Of splendour,
And life.

Future Generations

Longevity,
Ageless bodies,
Extraordinary minds.
The quest to be stronger,
Smarter, faster, to live longer.
Medically modified mind and body.
Merchandise owned by an industry,
A commodity, software, wired within;
Altered, linked, plugged to a hub;
A product of misconception.
No longer has its freedom,
Longing to stay alive.
Tinkered machinery,
Superfluous,
Tricked.

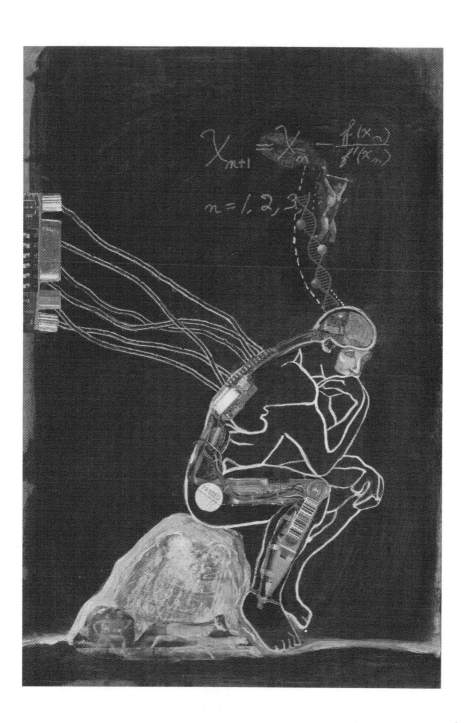

Freeing

Open your heart,
To its boundless possibilities.
Ideas for humanity to move forward
The breathless wonders of new insights,
Shedding old paradigms that constrict
Shackles, labels, separates, ostracise.
Your mind will soon follow
As your soul see through
With different eyes
Lighting the way,
Setting you free.

Chords of Light

Your heart
Is an instrument
Delicately tailored perfectly
To strum unique chords of light—
Like a cello that plays its event-strings
Beyond the understanding of the flesh
As melodies penetrate deeply,
Breaking all the chains
Of relentless despair
Throughout.

Invisible Threads

We are all multifaceted
Fragments and aspects

Of all that is known
And the unknown

Yet to be discovered,
As we remember the tracks

Left by our future selves
Bled through the arrow of time,

Danced by entanglement,
The meshing of invisible threads

Within the physical and ethereal,
The seen and unseen.

Complete

Endless
Is this beauteous dream,
Experiencing myriad sensations.
Awareness, irreplaceable waking moments,
Countless cycles and presence of being,
Feeling deep gratitude for such a gift.
Treasured soul adventures,
Innumerable tapestries
In culmination,
Complete
One.

Clues Left Behind

Within every image,
There is a different angle.
It has varied points of views
So we can see through darkness
Just by opening our eyes to light
To cross unchartered territories,
Past rivers in other stars,
Picking up the clues,
Remnants left behind
By our souls.

Avian

From a dream
Of a dream, Winged beings whispered
Ever so softly.

You already know
Your inner calling;
The words are written
In your heart.

Sing the songs.
Dance the dance.
Drum the drums.
Light the light.

For as you think,
You are already creating
And allowing your future resonant
To step into the now.

Watcher of Time

There's a time for fun,
A time for stillness,
And all that's in between.
Yet time does not wait for anyone.
Every minute forward turns into ...

Hours,
Days,
Weeks,
Months,
Years gone by.

We can do so much with time.
Don't just watch it pass you by,
And don't let time
Just watch us
Pass by.

Pockets Full of Stars

Pockets full of stars
Filled with the jewels
Of the cosmos
Are shimmering
Deep within.

Stored in memories,
Are light-trails
Carried through time,
Precious gems
Expressed by the soul.

Reflections

The heavens opened
Its arms of wondrousness

That stretch beyond
The multitude of stars,

We gaze deeply
Into its heart,

Only to find
Its reflections

Within
Our own.

In the Distant Future

Looking back
At the place where we came from—
A haven, our home.

Some called it Mother Earth
Those many centuries ago,
Filled with lush, thriving life.

A place with clear, blue skies
Swooping birds, butterflies, fresh air,
Calm rivers, and wild seas.

Now it is barren,
A wasteland with toxic rain,
A withering shell.

Remnants of a great civilisation
Blowing in the wind,
Dissipating before its time.

Nothing has remained
To say we were there
As we look back from afar.

In our adventures
Light years away,
We cultivate yet another terrain

During our quest to sustain
Humanity's lineage
Through the frontiers of space and heart.

Dreamscape

In every star,
There exist

Dreamscapes
Ready to be experienced.

Just as in each being
Are remnants of stars

Danced into form
By dream carriers.

Journey's Bound

Life is a journey
With its twist and turns;
Takes us to highs and lows.
Destinations of the heart,
Adventures unknown,
A manuscript unfolding
Within the soul.

Star Gate

There's a point
Where dark matter
Is shattered by blinding light,
And its darkness
Coalesces into form,

Pouring forth a kaleidoscope of colours—
Remnants of star dust
Reforming into spheres of new realities
With unimaginable landscapes
Beyond the current realms,

Waking the guardians
That open gateways in space—
Passages without linear time,
Portals to new worlds
In other universes.

Woken From a Dream

We opened our eyes
And found that we are here,
In a world within another dream.
Enfolded by countless of dimensions
All occurring at the same time,
Coexisting in a multiverse.

So much yet to behold
As many layers of realms,
Are spliced within the unseen,
Unfathomable by our understanding.
But as we awaken from our prism
We can clearly see, beyond the chrysalis of being.

Contemplations

Here,
Momentarily,

I am

The inner self
In search for clues,

Poised

In contemplation,
Anticipating the directions

Of my soul.

More Than Words

Words cannot describe
The feeling of utmost peace

That fills and surrounds me
As my presence merges with all,

Enfolded by absolute love
In this place of boundlessness.

Words cannot express
The totality,

Completeness,
Joy.

Other Side

Alive,
Filled with life force,

Experiencing existence through flesh.
But as time stood still,

That which is beyond,
The imagination,

Has now
Begun.

Art Acknowledgement

Deepest gratitude to Belinda Green and Teka Luttrell for providing their amazing art work for this project of creation.

Belinda Green

www.belindagreenart.blogspot.com.au
www.facebook.com/belindagreenart

Teka Luttrell
The Soul Connection Network

www.soulconnection.net

Art References

Front and back Page Image:
Image taken by NASA's Hubble telescope of galaxies in deep space. Public domain. Created by _NASA_ and _ESA_.

Front Page:
Image titled "Cosmic Self Be True" by Teka Luttell

* **1st image** – pg 3. Titled "More Than A Shadow" by Belinda Green

* **2nd image** – pg 9. Titled Dear Butterfly by Maridol Torres for the poem "Dear Butterfly."

* **3rd image** – pg 17. Titled Dream keeper by Belinda Green for the poem "Dream keeper."

* **4th image** – pg 25. Titled Seer by Belinda Green for the poem "Seer."

* **5th image** – pg 35. Titled Phoenix by Maridol Torres for the poem "Phoenix."

* **6th image** – pg 43. Titled Going Before Your Time by Belinda Green for the poem "Going Before Your Time."

* **7th image** – pg 51. Titled Beside You by Maridol Torres for the poem "Beside You."

* **8th image** – pg 62. Titled Secrets Of Time by Belinda Green for the poem "Secrets Of Time."

* **9th image** – pg 73. Titled Other Worlds by Belinda Green for poem "Other Wolds."

Notes

Printed in the United States
By Bookmasters